# Prison Segmentation for Video Notes

I0492804

# For Spouses and Children

Reverend Mike Wanner

-

# Table of Contents

# 1 - Why I am Writing This Book

Communications are crucial in today's world to family bonding, but prisoners are not high on the list of those being able to access the communication technology.

Prisoners families probably need the boost from video more than intact families, and I would like to explore here some ideas which might help.

Children feel the loss of their parents. My dad died when I was eleven. Messages can make a difference. He could not send any, but you might be able to.

I once had a friend who divorced her husband for a just reason. One issue was that he had no time for his son.

The young man worked hard at his studies and his physical conditioning, but his father was not interested, and dad was free and able just to make a call, but he did not do it. At age twenty-one, the good-looking young man committed suicide because his heart was not as happy as his body.

Parents can make a real difference in the lives of their children.

2 - Families Upside Down is Terrible

Prisoners' Spouses Have It Tough

Families Flipped Over Come in Every Shape
and Size and Color and Culture

Your Absence Hurts

3 - Your Family is Feeling the Loss

Communication is Not Easy

Positive Thinking Can Help

Avoid Down Spiral Thinking

Choose Uplifting Thinking

Consider Sending Prayers of Love
The Delivery Will Not Be Impeded

Develop Your Ability to Visualize
A Better Future

See Problems Dissolve in Your Future

Communicate As Best You Can

# 4 - Your Spouse Partner

## May Feel Like A Part of Their Life is Amputated

## Their Joy Is Cut in Half

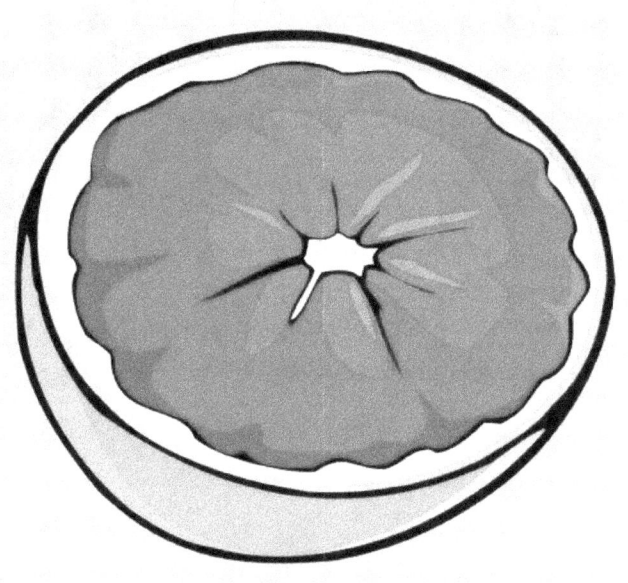

## Their Peace has Left the Body

# 5 - Demands on Your Spouse May be Huge

## So Much To Do!

1.
2.
3.
4.
5.
6.

# 6 - Spouses Are Special

## They Need to Hear It

## They Need to Know It

## They Need To Feel It

## They Need To Believe It

# 7 - Dads or Moms May be In Prison

## Children still need encouragement

Kids Can Repay Encouragement with Encouragement!

8 - Children May Understand If Told

They May Be Sad

You Can Help!

Will You?

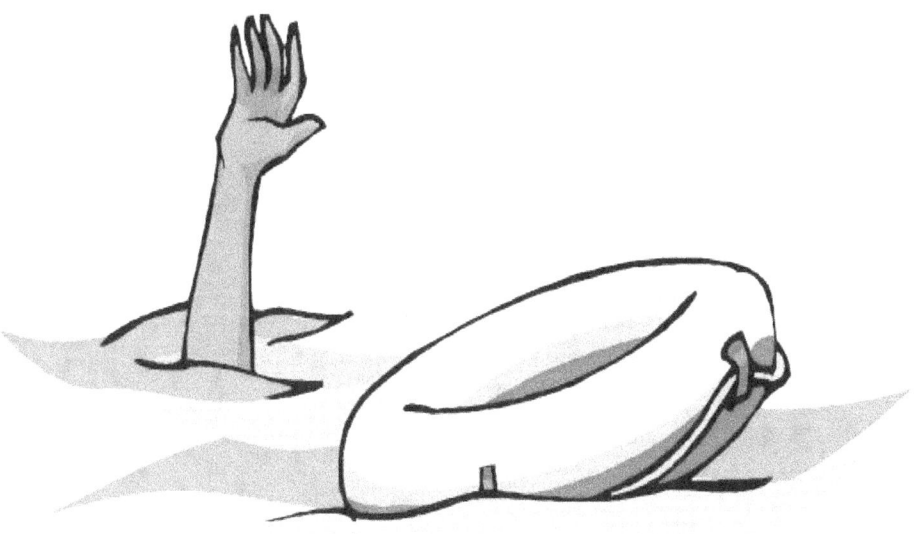

Talk - Message – Speak

Your Words Matter

9 - Children Need Love & Joy

Your Children Can Still be Blessed
by Your Joy

You Can Find Some Joy in Your Memories
And Share It

You Can Say Things
that Heal Your Children
& Also the Child in You

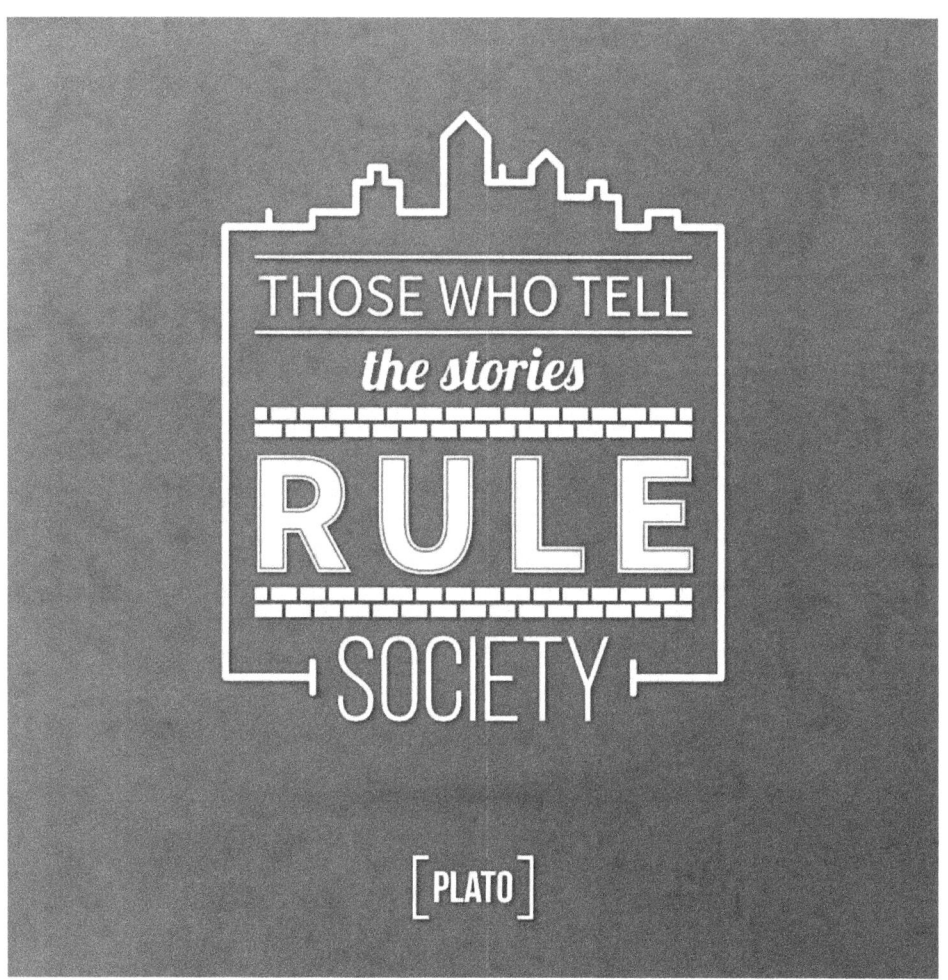

THOSE WHO TELL
*the stories*
RULE
SOCIETY

[ PLATO ]

# 11 - Tell About Obeying Parent or Guardian

# 12 - Tell About Obeying Teachers

# 13 - Tell About Studying and Doing Well

# 14 - Tell About Getting Along with Others

# 15 - Tell About Being Kind to Others

# 16 - A Lot Can Be in The Way

Visitation Policies

Depressing Environment

Less Than Friendly Acquaintances

Communication Access Limitations

Not Seeing the Child

Delays

# 17 - You Can Make A Plan

# &

# Get Started

# &

# Track Progress

Notes of all kinds and especially Video Notes can help keep things in perspective and provide an open line of communication. Help ensure maximum interactions with your family. A little bit can go a long way when it is done well.

# 18 - Video Can Really Help

YouTube has made an impact, and it may be an excellent tool for prisons to adopt for a number of reasons. Video can:

1. Say a lot without saying a lot.

2. Control the presentation of the message.

3. Be light and uplifting.

4. Be economical to oversee.

5. Fulfill deep needs for prisoner interacting with their children.

6. Fulfill deep needs for prisoner interacting with their spouses.

7. Fulfill deep needs for prisoner interacting with their potential employers.

8. Fulfill deep needs for prisoner interacting with their extended families.

9. Fulfill deep needs for prisoner interacting with their business colleagues and potential customers.

# 19 - Staging

The quality of the video will not be initially as crucial as the staging. Ideally, the initial work will be to design some sets that are:

1. Family Friendly

2. Spouse Friendly

3. Child-Friendly

4. Extended Family Friendly

5. Employment seeking Friendly

6. Fellow Prisoner Friendly

7. Hope Friendly

8. Bonding Friendly

9. Re-Unification Friendly

10. RE-Entry Friendly

# 20 - Foundation Building

Children who are growing up move pretty fast and long sentences can have a lot that is missed. Capturing the story and energy and emotion of the growing up process will not replace the experience that one could have if they were free but it helps.

Maintaining perspective for both prisoners and their children can go a long way to keep the bond alive between parent and child so that there is not a disconnect permanently.

You May Understand Your Situation, but you have not walked in the shoes of your child and ignoring their situation is not helpful to you or them. Doing what you will can help you both understand and relate.

Your outreach will be noticed and bring aliveness to your heart connection that may trigger much more to stifle isolation and emotional shutdown.

Maturity can also evolve from your efforts toward proper responsible behavior. The experience can carry a bounty of understanding for many other people and things in a way that invigorates your feelings of value and aliveness.

You may think that your life situation may not be fixable and you may be right or wrong. Knowing for sure how you feel will be a great benefit to your self-image and self-peace.

It may take A Lot of Effort, but the work may be a salve for a wounded heart.

# 21 - Know You Can:

Be Kind & Great

Release Fear & Hate

You Can Like Others,
So They Like You

Shine Bright
Your Light

Share Your Light & Joy

Be An Example
So The Ones who Watch You,
May Shine Too

## Know that:

Father God Knows - Who You Are

When You Serve Other, God Serves You Also!

# 22 - How to Bond with People

## 1. Auditorily

Talking to people is a beneficial way to communicate thoughts, hopes, dreams, and love.

## 2. Visually

Showing people is a very effective way to communicate thoughts, hopes, dreams, and love.

## 3. Kinesthetically

Kinesthetics (or touching People) is used to communicate thoughts, hopes, dreams, and love.

## All Three Is Best

If you cannot do all three, Video could do the first two much better than a paper note and can be replayed multiple times to increase the connection. The video should not be used in place of human contact but as an amplifier of human interactions and re-enlivening of past experiences and previously experienced bonds.

## Staging Is Important

Please reread Chapter 19 before creating each video.

For
Considering
These
Ideas

# It Does Not Help Prayer Still Does!

Resource: http://Create-A-Prayer.com

# 25 - Books Category Resources
## at www.Amazon.com

Distant Healing (or Mail List) e-mail mikewann@voicenet.com

Veterans Healing Six Pack plus 2
*http://angelraphaelspeaks.com/healing-books/veterans/*

PTSD Power Pack
*http://angelraphaelspeaks.com/healing-books/ptsd/*

Angel Raphael Speaks Series & Other Angel Books
*http://angelraphaelspeaks.com/*

Reiki
*http://angelraphaelspeaks.com/healing-books/reiki/*

Children
*http://angelraphaelspeaks.com/healing-books/children/*

Emergency Medical Kindness
*http://angelraphaelspeaks.com/healing-books/emergency-medical-kindness/*

Cancer
*http://angelraphaelspeaks.com/healing-books/cancer/*

*Addictions*
*http://angelraphaelspeaks.com/healing-books/addictions/*

Miscellaneous Healing
*http://angelraphaelspeaks.com/healing-books/misc-healing/*

Prison Books - 50+ Prison Books
http://angelraphaelspeaks.com/prison-books/

# 26 - Angels Please Prayers

### Addict's
Angels of Healing Selected
Help Me to Stay Directed
Come To Me From The Sky
I Am Ready to Succeed Not Try
If I Don't Invite You In
I Might Not Win
I Have Been Lost For Too Long
Help Me To Stay Strong

### Alcoholic's
Angels of Healing On High
Help Me to Stay Dry
Come To Me From The Sky
I Am Ready to Succeed Not Try
If I Don't Invite You In
I Might Not Win
I Have Been Lost For Too Long
Help Me To Stay Strong

From

http://AngelRaphaelSpeaks.com/AAAAAAA/
The Link Above Has the Core Messages from the book on drop-down pages.

# 27 - Private Channeling

Angel Raphael Speaks a series of free messages that are channeled through Reverend Mike Wanner for the Highest good and Highest Healing of all concerned.

Many questions arise about Reverend Mike doing private channeling, and he does help with that so E-mail him.

Reverend Mike is available worldwide as a psychic channel, emotional release facilitator, spiritual energy practitioner & teacher, and public speaker. He looks forward to meeting you soon! Email - mikewann@voicenet.com 215-342-1270

PRIVATE SPIRITUAL READINGS/channelings or Spiritual Healing Sessions: Telephone or in person.

Rev. Mike is available for individual, intuitive one-on-one sessions with you, his Guide Family, and your Guides. He helps by offering clarity on emotional situations about your life, your purpose, your spirituality, and your release of stuffed emotions and cellular memory.

Connect to the love of your Guides today!

For more information, Please visit

http://angelraphaelspeaks.com/channel/

# 28 - Reverend Mike Wanner

Rev. Mike Wanner started his spiritual and ministerial studies with Reiki in 1993 and had studied seven styles of Reiki in the U.S., Japan, Canada, Denmark and Australia. He is certified to teach.

He became certified to teach Integrated Energy Therapy in 1999 and co-taught the first IET class of the new Millennium. Mike began dowsing in 2001.

Ordained as an Interfaith Minister of the Circle of Miracles Ministry and a Metaphysical Minister of the International Metaphysical Ministry, Rev. Mike practices and teaches spiritual energy therapies in the Philadelphia Area.

Rev. Mike holds ministerial degrees from the University of Metaphysics and the University of Sedona. He is a Pastoral Care Associate at Jefferson - Frankford Hospital. He taught at the National Academy of Massage Therapy and Health Sciences.

Rev. Mike was a faculty member of the Medical Mission Sister's Center for Human Integration's School of Integrated Body/Mind Therapies in Fox Chase, Philadelphia, PA for twelve years.

For a complete Biography, Please visit
http://ReverendMikeWanner.com/Bio